·My·First·
Atlas

Library of Congress Cataloging-in-Publication Data

Snow, Alan.
    My first atlas / illustrated by Alan Snow.
      p.   cm.
    Summary: Maps and text introduce the continents and countries of
the world, describing their climate, animal life, and other
significant features.
    ISBN 0-8167-2517-9 (lib. bdg.)   ISBN 0-8167-2518-7 (pbk.)
    1. Atlases. [1. Atlases.] I. Snow, Alan, ill. II. Troll
Associates.
G1021.M8 1992
912—dc20
                                91-24303

Published by Troll Associates.
Copyright © 1992 Joshua Morris Publishing Inc.
and Alan Snow.
Illustrations © 1991 Alan Snow.
Text by Times Four Publishing Ltd.
Printed in Singapore.
10 9 8 7 6 5 4 3 2 1

·My·First·
Atlas

Illustrated by
Alan
Snow

Troll Associates

Contents

What Is an Atlas?

Imagine trying to hold up the sky on your shoulders! According to a very old Greek story, that's what a giant named Atlas was forced to do. Atlas and some other giants were called Titans. They fought Zeus, the king of the gods, and the gods loyal to Zeus. But the Titans lost the war, and Zeus punished Atlas by making him stand with the sky on his shoulders.

Pictures of Atlas holding up the sky often appeared in early books of maps. After a while, people started calling these books *atlases*. The word *atlas* has been used to describe a book of maps ever since.

My First Atlas has maps of North America, South America, Europe, Asia, Africa, USSR, the Arctic, and other large land areas. It also has fascinating facts and figures about the people, animals, cities, mountains, lakes, and products found in each area. And at the back of the book you will find **Atlas Fun**, where you can test your knowledge of the world.

North America

Canada, the United States of America, Mexico, and the Caribbean region are all part of North America.

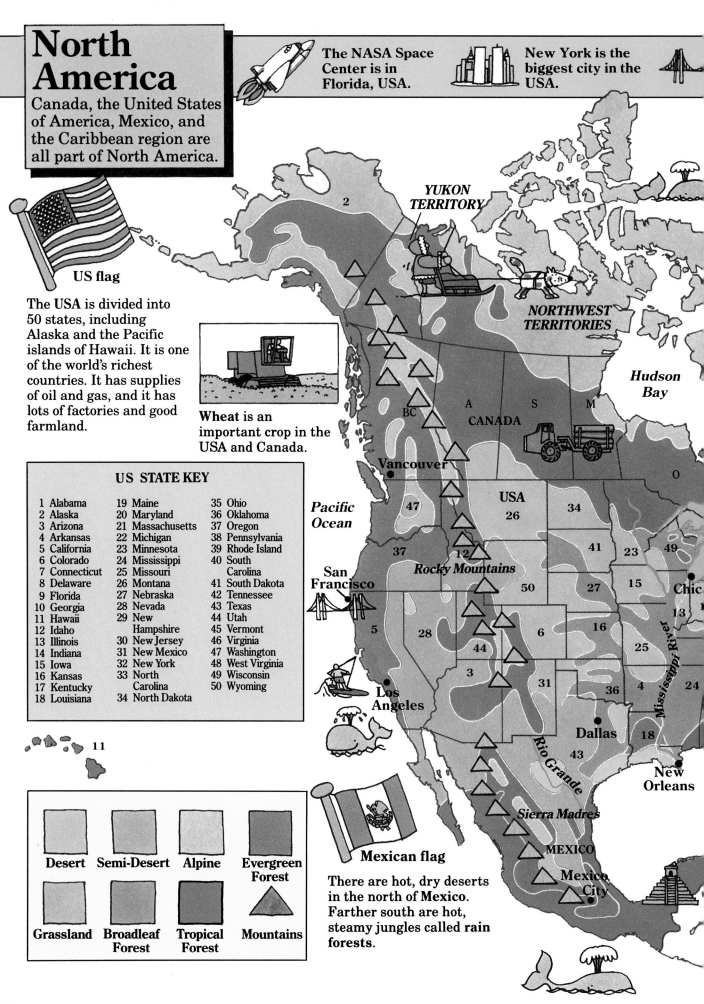

US flag

The USA is divided into 50 states, including Alaska and the Pacific islands of Hawaii. It is one of the world's richest countries. It has supplies of oil and gas, and it has lots of factories and good farmland.

Wheat is an important crop in the USA and Canada.

US STATE KEY

1 Alabama	19 Maine	35 Ohio
2 Alaska	20 Maryland	36 Oklahoma
3 Arizona	21 Massachusetts	37 Oregon
4 Arkansas	22 Michigan	38 Pennsylvania
5 California	23 Minnesota	39 Rhode Island
6 Colorado	24 Mississippi	40 South
7 Connecticut	25 Missouri	Carolina
8 Delaware	26 Montana	41 South Dakota
9 Florida	27 Nebraska	42 Tennessee
10 Georgia	28 Nevada	43 Texas
11 Hawaii	29 New	44 Utah
12 Idaho	Hampshire	45 Vermont
13 Illinois	30 New Jersey	46 Virginia
14 Indiana	31 New Mexico	47 Washington
15 Iowa	32 New York	48 West Virginia
16 Kansas	33 North	49 Wisconsin
17 Kentucky	Carolina	50 Wyoming
18 Louisiana	34 North Dakota	

Desert **Semi-Desert** **Alpine** **Evergreen Forest**

Grassland **Broadleaf Forest** **Tropical Forest** **Mountains**

Mexican flag

There are hot, dry deserts in the north of **Mexico**. Farther south are hot, steamy jungles called **rain forests**.

NORTH
AMERICA

famous Golden
Bridge is
n Francisco.

The ancient Mayans
once built cities in
Mexico.

High mountains run all the way down the west coast. In Canada and the USA, they are known as the **Rocky Mountains.** In Mexico, they are known as the **Sierra Madres.**

Canadian flag

Canada is the world's second largest country in area. In the north it has many lakes and forests where elk, moose, deer, and wolves live. In the south it has flat lands where farmers grow wheat and other crops.

Canadian mountain scenery

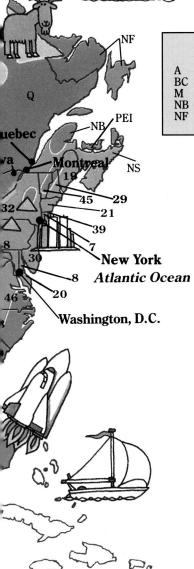

NF

Q

Quebec
va

Montreal
19

45 — 29
21
39
7
New York
Atlantic Ocean
8
20

Washington, D.C.

NB PEI
NB
NS

32
△
△
8
30
46

CANADIAN PROVINCE KEY

A	Alberta	NS	Nova Scotia
BC	British Columbia	O	Ontario
M	Manitoba	PEI	Prince Edward Island
NB	New Brunswick	Q	Quebec
NF	Newfoundland	S	Saskatchewan

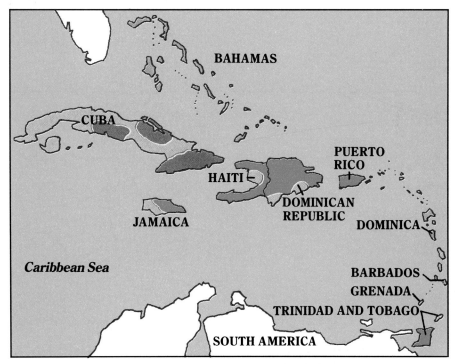

BAHAMAS

CUBA

PUERTO
RICO

HAITI

DOMINICAN
REPUBLIC

DOMINICA

JAMAICA

Caribbean Sea

BARBADOS
GRENADA
TRINIDAD AND TOBAGO

SOUTH AMERICA

Caribbean Sea

The Caribbean Sea is an arm of the Atlantic Ocean off the coast of mainland North America. Cuba and the Dominican Republic are here, along with many other islands. The climate is very warm, and the area is a popular place for tourists to visit. The hot weather is good for growing sugar cane and bananas. However, sometimes hurricanes sweep over the land and cause lots of damage.

Central and South America

The continent of South America is about 4,500 miles (7,241 kilometers) long. It has deserts, rain forests, mountains, and grasslands. Central America is the thin piece of land that joins Mexico to South America.

High in the Peruvian Andes sits the ancient city of Machu Picchu.

Fierce piranha fish live in the Amazon River.

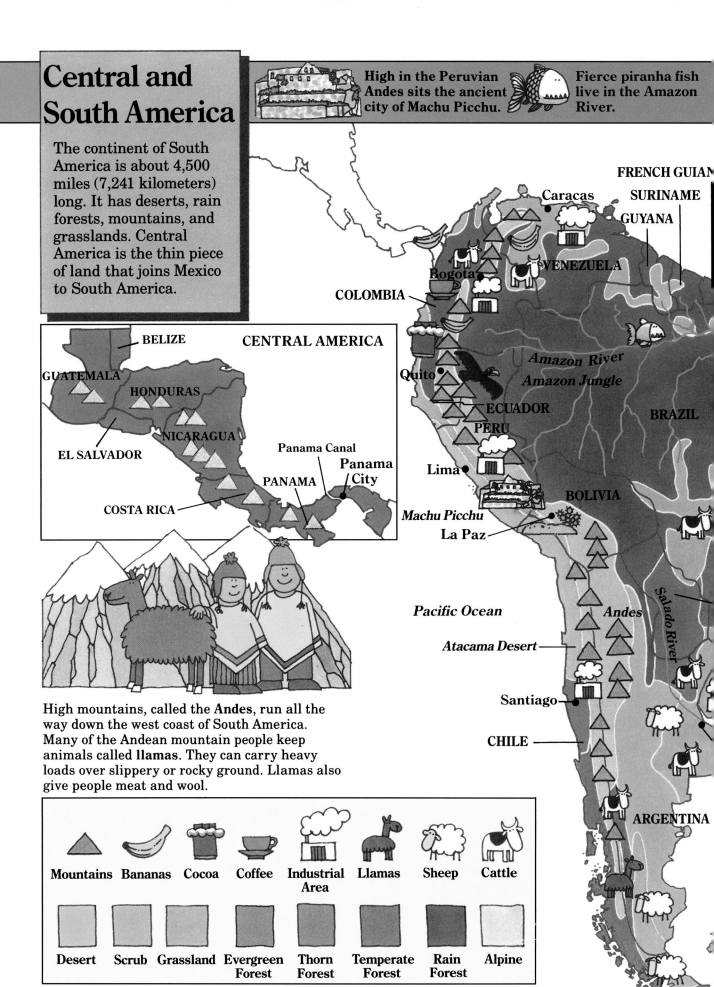

CENTRAL AMERICA

BELIZE
GUATEMALA
HONDURAS
EL SALVADOR
NICARAGUA
COSTA RICA
PANAMA
Panama Canal
Panama City

FRENCH GUIANA
SURINAME
GUYANA
Caracas
VENEZUELA
Bogota
COLOMBIA
Quito
ECUADOR
PERU
Lima
BOLIVIA
Machu Picchu
La Paz
Amazon River
Amazon Jungle
BRAZIL
Salado River
Pacific Ocean
Andes
Atacama Desert
Santiago
CHILE
ARGENTINA

High mountains, called the **Andes**, run all the way down the west coast of South America. Many of the Andean mountain people keep animals called **llamas**. They can carry heavy loads over slippery or rocky ground. Llamas also give people meat and wool.

Mountains Bananas Cocoa Coffee Industrial Area Llamas Sheep Cattle

Desert Scrub Grassland Evergreen Forest Thorn Forest Temperate Forest Rain Forest Alpine

THE WORLD

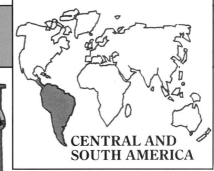

CENTRAL AND SOUTH AMERICA

The first **South American people** were American Indians. Then people from Spain, Portugal, and Africa came to live there. Many of the people living there today are a mixture of races.

Early American Indian objects

Atlantic Ocean

There are still some **Indian tribes** living in the South American jungles. They survive by hunting animals and eating jungle plants.

Brazilian flag

More than half of Brazil is covered by hot steamy jungle called rain forest. It grows around the **Amazon,** which is one of the biggest rivers in the world. The Amazon begins in the Andes mountains and flows all the way across Brazil to the Atlantic Ocean. Large boats can sail only part of the way up the river. After that, the best way to travel is by smaller boats such as canoes.

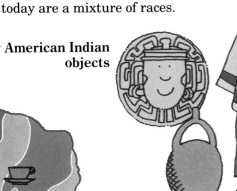

silia

Rio de Janeiro

PARAGUAY

Lots of **animals and plants** live in the rain forest. But their home is threatened because large parts of the forest are being chopped down. Many people are trying to stop this from happening because the forests are important to everybody in the world. The trees help to clean the air and make it better for everyone to breathe. Here are some rain forest animals:

RUGUAY

tevideo

nos Aires

Macaw

Hummingbird

Howler monkey

Toucan

Sloth

Jaguar

Caiman

kland Islands

Northern Europe

Europe stretches from the cold Arctic Ocean in the north to the hot lands around the Mediterranean. This map shows the northern part of Europe. The area in the far north is called Scandinavia.

In the far north are herds of reindeer.

One of London's most famous sights is the Tower of Lon...

British flag

Scandinavia includes Norway, Sweden, and Denmark. Much of northern Scandinavia is covered with **forests** of fir trees. They are cut down and used for making paper and other wood products.

Norwegian flag

Fishing is important around the coastline of northern Europe.

There are many **factories** in northern Europe. Some of them are used for making machinery such as cars, trucks, and TVs. There are coal mines and steel-making plants, too.

Ar

ICELAND

•Reykjavik

Iceland is an island country with glaciers, hot springs and volcanoes.

The United Kingdom is made up of Scotland, Wales, England, and Northern Ireland. The capital city is London.

NORWAY

Atlantic Ocean

North Sea

SCOTLAND (UK)

Glasgow

Edinburgh

DENMA...

NORTHERN IRELAND (UK)

REPUBLIC OF IRELAND   Belfast

Dublin

UNITED KINGDOM

Hamb...

ENGLAND (UK)

Rhine River

Bonn

WALES (UK)

London

GERMANY

In **the Republic of Ireland** the land is mainly used for farming. There is plenty of good fishing around the coasts.

LIECHTENSTEIN

10

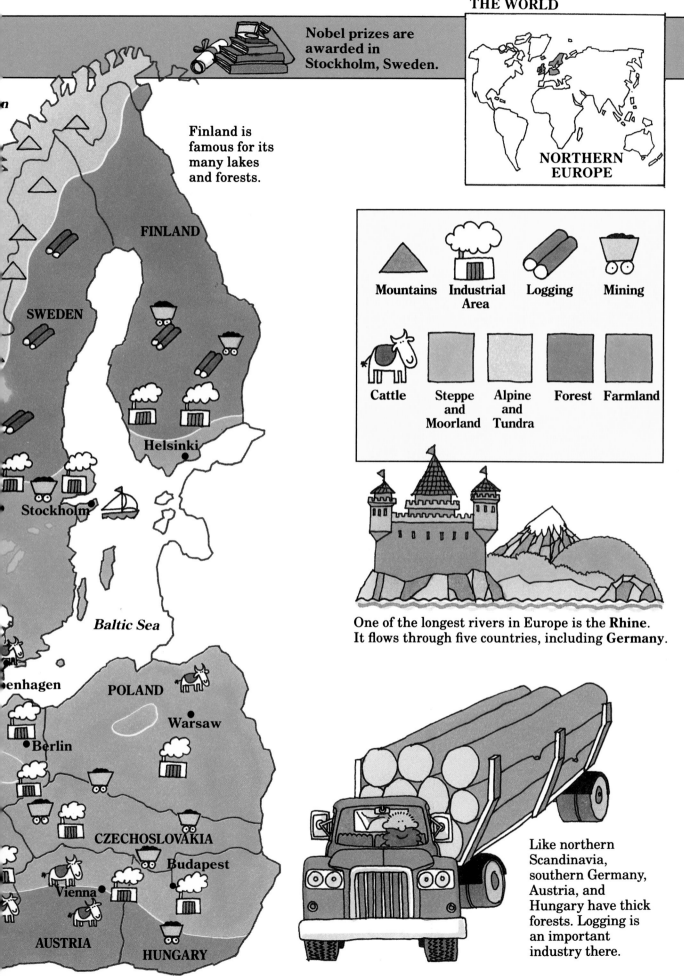

NORTHERN EUROPE

Nobel prizes are awarded in Stockholm, Sweden.

Finland is famous for its many lakes and forests.

FINLAND

SWEDEN

Helsinki

Stockholm

Baltic Sea

enhagen

POLAND

Warsaw

Berlin

CZECHOSLOVAKIA

Budapest

Vienna

AUSTRIA

HUNGARY

Legend:

Mountains | Industrial Area | Logging | Mining

Cattle | Steppe and Moorland | Alpine and Tundra | Forest | Farmland

One of the longest rivers in Europe is the **Rhine**. It flows through five countries, including **Germany**.

Like northern Scandinavia, southern Germany, Austria, and Hungary have thick forests. Logging is an important industry there.

Southern Europe

The countries in the southern part of Europe are hot and sunny in summertime. The southern coastline is beside the warm Mediterranean Sea. It has lots of popular summer holiday resorts.

The **Netherlands** is a very flat country. Much of the land was once covered by sea, but Dutch engineers have drained away the water and built dams called **dikes** to keep it out. The drained areas of land are called **polders**.

NETHERLANDS

Amsterdam

Rotterdam

Brussels
BELGIUM

LUXEMBOURG
Paris *Seine River*

The countries around the Mediterranean have a warm climate that is good for **farming.** Many farmers in Spain, France, and Italy grow grapes and olives. The warm weather is also good for growing fruit such as oranges and lemons.

Atlantic Ocean

FRANCE

Bay of Biscay

Lyon

Swiss flag

In Switzerland there are high mountains called the **Alps.** They are popular for skiing.

ANDOR

Spanish flag

More tourists visit **Spain** than any other European country. It has lots of sandy beaches.

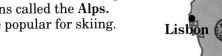

PORTUGAL

Madrid

SPAIN

Majorca

Lisbon

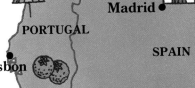

AFRICA

Venice, Italy, has canals through it instead of roads.

Mont Blanc in France is the highest point in the Alps.

THE WORLD

SOUTHERN EUROPE

About two thousand years ago the **Romans** conquered southern Europe. You can still see the remains of their cities. They built Rome, capital of Italy.

Italian flag

SWITZERLAND
Zurich

SLOVENIA
CROATIA
SERBIA
YUGOSLAVIA
BOSNIA AND HERCEGOVINA
MONTENEGRO
MACEDONIA

ROMANIA
Bucharest

Black Sea

BULGARIA
Sofia

TURKEY
Istanbul

Venice

eneva

NACO

Corsica

Sardinia

diterranean Sea

San Marino

Adriatic Sea

Rome

ITALY

ALBANIA

GREECE

Aegean Sea

TURKEY

Athens

Sicily

MALTA

Crete

Industrial Area | **Citrus Fruit** | **Holiday Resort** | **Grapes** | **Mountains** | **Skiing** | **Apples**

Alpine | **Coniferous Forest** | **Evergreen Forest** | **Broadleaf Forest** | **Grassland** | **Steppe and Semi-Desert**

Africa

Africa is a huge continent divided into many countries. There are deserts in the north and south, where very little rain falls. In the middle are hot rain forests.

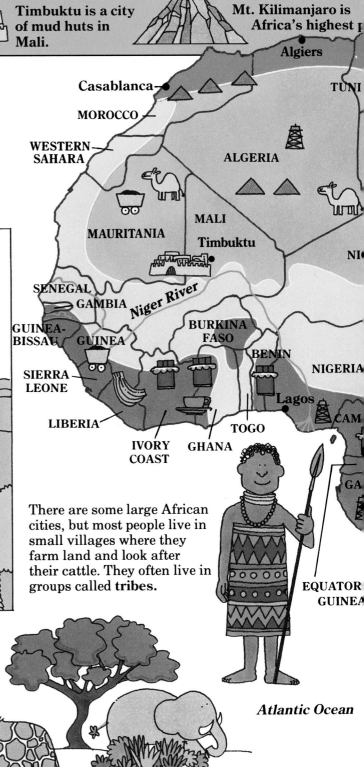

Timbuktu is a city of mud huts in Mali.

Mt. Kilimanjaro is Africa's highest

Algiers

Casablanca

TUNI

MOROCCO

WESTERN SAHARA

ALGERIA

MAURITANIA

MALI

Timbuktu

NI

SENEGAL

GAMBIA

Niger River

GUINEA-BISSAU

GUINEA

BURKINA FASO

BENIN

NIGERIA

SIERRA LEONE

LIBERIA

IVORY COAST

GHANA

TOGO

Lagos

CAM

GA

EQUATOR

GUINEA

Atlantic Ocean

The **Sahara Desert,** in North Africa, is the largest desert in the world. During the day it is very hot, but at night it is cold. The Saharan people use camels for travel over the sand. The camels can go for days without water.

There are some large African cities, but most people live in small villages where they farm land and look after their cattle. They often live in groups called **tribes.**

There are wide grassy plains called **grasslands** in Africa. Herds of wild animals wander over the grasslands in search of food. Zebras, elephants, and giraffes eat the leaves of the trees and bushes. Lions and cheetahs hunt the plant-eating animals.

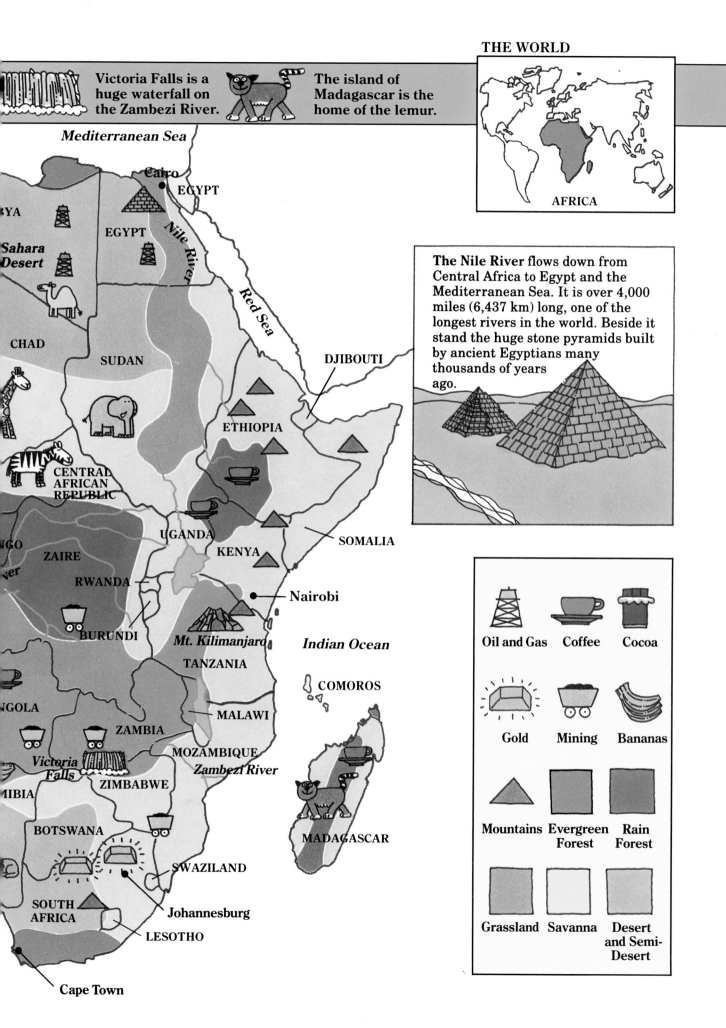

Victoria Falls is a huge waterfall on the Zambezi River.

The island of Madagascar is the home of the lemur.

THE WORLD

AFRICA

Mediterranean Sea

Cairo
EGYPT
EGYPT
Nile River

Sahara Desert

CHAD

SUDAN

Red Sea

DJIBOUTI

ETHIOPIA

SOMALIA

CENTRAL AFRICAN REPUBLIC

UGANDA

ZAIRE

KENYA

RWANDA

Nairobi

BURUNDI

Mt. Kilimanjaro

Indian Ocean

TANZANIA

COMOROS

NGOLA

MALAWI

ZAMBIA

MOZAMBIQUE

Victoria Falls

Zambezi River

ZIMBABWE

MIBIA

BOTSWANA

MADAGASCAR

SWAZILAND

SOUTH AFRICA

Johannesburg

LESOTHO

Cape Town

The Nile River flows down from Central Africa to Egypt and the Mediterranean Sea. It is over 4,000 miles (6,437 km) long, one of the longest rivers in the world. Beside it stand the huge stone pyramids built by ancient Egyptians many thousands of years ago.

Oil and Gas   Coffee   Cocoa

Gold   Mining   Bananas

Mountains   Evergreen Forest   Rain Forest

Grassland   Savanna   Desert and Semi-Desert

15

USSR

The USSR (the Soviet Union) is the world's largest country in area. The western part is in Europe. The eastern part, beyond the Ural Mountains, is in Asia.

The deepest lake in the world is Lake Baikal, in Central Siberia.

Many Soviet churches have round, onion like domes.

About a third of the USSR is covered in **forests**. Elk, deer, and bears are some of the animals found there.

In some areas the trees are cut into logs to make wooden products and paper.

Ar●
Oc●

In 1991, radical changes began sweeping the Soviet Union. Many republics declared independence.

The USSR is sometimes called **Russia,** but Russia is only a part of the country. There are many different kinds of people in the Soviet Union, and more than 100 languages.

In the south of the USSR are **deserts** where few plants grow and very few people live.

Murmansk

Ural Mountains

Volga River

Ob River

RUSSIA

St. Petersburg
ESTONIA
LATVIA
LITHUANIA
RSFSR
Tallinn
Riga
Moscow
Vilnius
BYELORUSSIA

Kiev

KAZAKH

UKRAINE
MOLDAVIA
Odessa

Black Sea

GEORGIA

ARMENIA
AZERBAIJAN

Caspian Sea

UZBEK
Tashkent

KIRG

TURKMEN

TADZH

Between the forests and the deserts are vast, flat, grassy plains called **steppes.** This land is good for growing wheat and other crops.

16

The Kremlin in Moscow houses a famous museum.

The Trans-Siberian Railroad is the longest in the world.

USSR

In the north of the country are huge areas where it is so cold that the ground is frozen for most of the year. These parts are called **tundra**. Herds of reindeer live there.

The northeast part of the area called **Siberia** is famous for its freezing winters.

Part of the USSR is inside the **Arctic Circle,** an imaginary line drawn on maps around the North Pole. Inside the circle it is always very cold.

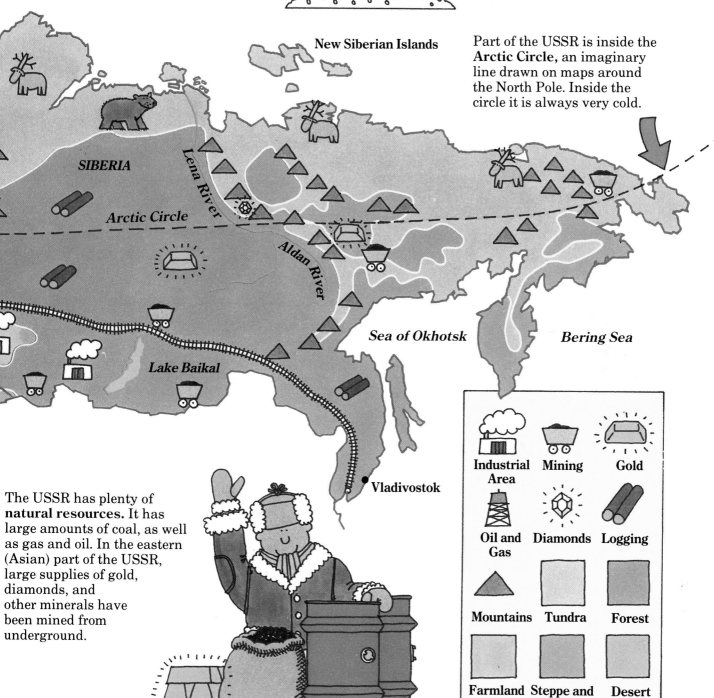

New Siberian Islands

SIBERIA

Lena River

Arctic Circle

Aldan River

Sea of Okhotsk

Bering Sea

Lake Baikal

• **Vladivostok**

The USSR has plenty of **natural resources.** It has large amounts of coal, as well as gas and oil. In the eastern (Asian) part of the USSR, large supplies of gold, diamonds, and other minerals have been mined from underground.

Industrial Area	**Mining**	**Gold**
Oil and Gas	**Diamonds**	**Logging**
Mountains	**Tundra**	**Forest**
Farmland	**Steppe and Semi-Desert**	**Desert**

Asia (1)

Asia is a huge continent stretching from the Mediterranean Sea to the Pacific Ocean. More than half the world's people live there. This map shows the Middle East and southern Asia.

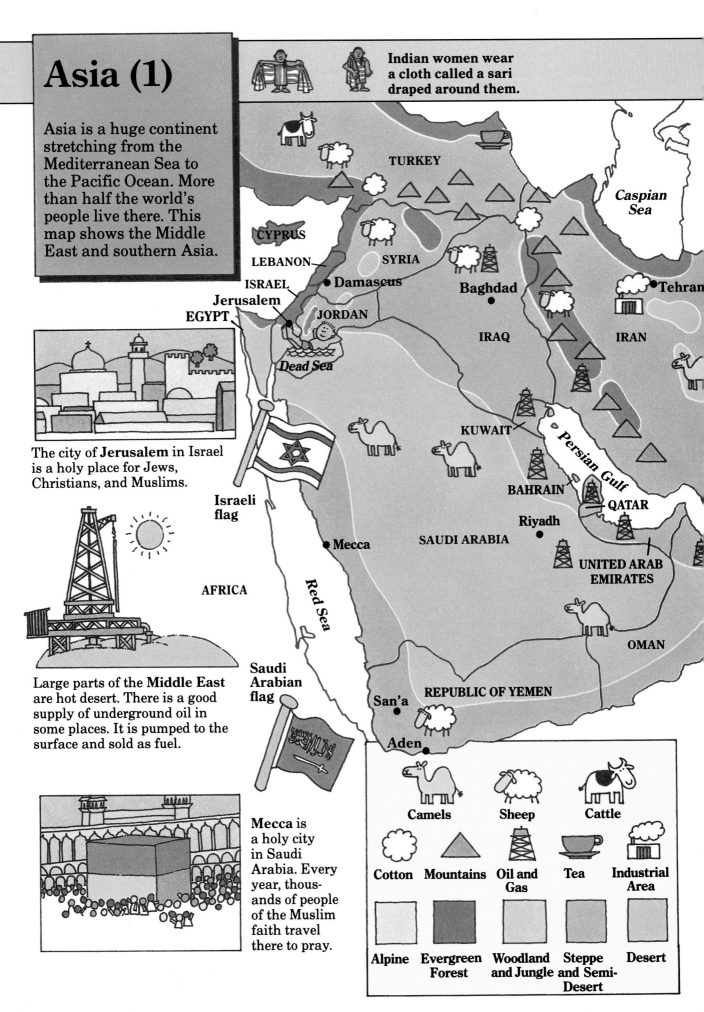

Indian women wear a cloth called a sari draped around them.

The city of **Jerusalem** in Israel is a holy place for Jews, Christians, and Muslims.

Israeli flag

Large parts of the **Middle East** are hot desert. There is a good supply of underground oil in some places. It is pumped to the surface and sold as fuel.

Saudi Arabian flag

Mecca is a holy city in Saudi Arabia. Every year, thousands of people of the Muslim faith travel there to pray.

TURKEY

CYPRUS

LEBANON

ISRAEL

Jerusalem

EGYPT

Damascus

SYRIA

JORDAN

Dead Sea

Baghdad

IRAQ

Caspian Sea

Tehran

IRAN

KUWAIT

Persian Gulf

BAHRAIN

QATAR

Riyadh

SAUDI ARABIA

UNITED ARAB EMIRATES

AFRICA

Mecca

Red Sea

OMAN

REPUBLIC OF YEMEN

San'a

Aden

Camels **Sheep** **Cattle**

Cotton **Mountains** **Oil and Gas** **Tea** **Industrial Area**

Alpine **Evergreen Forest** **Woodland and Jungle** **Steppe and Semi-Desert** **Desert**

18

India's Taj Mahal building is famous for its beauty.

The Dead Sea is so salty that you can float on top of it.

The **Himalayas** are huge mountains that run across the north of India. One of them is Mount Everest, the highest mountain in the world. It is more than 5 miles (8,839 meters) high.

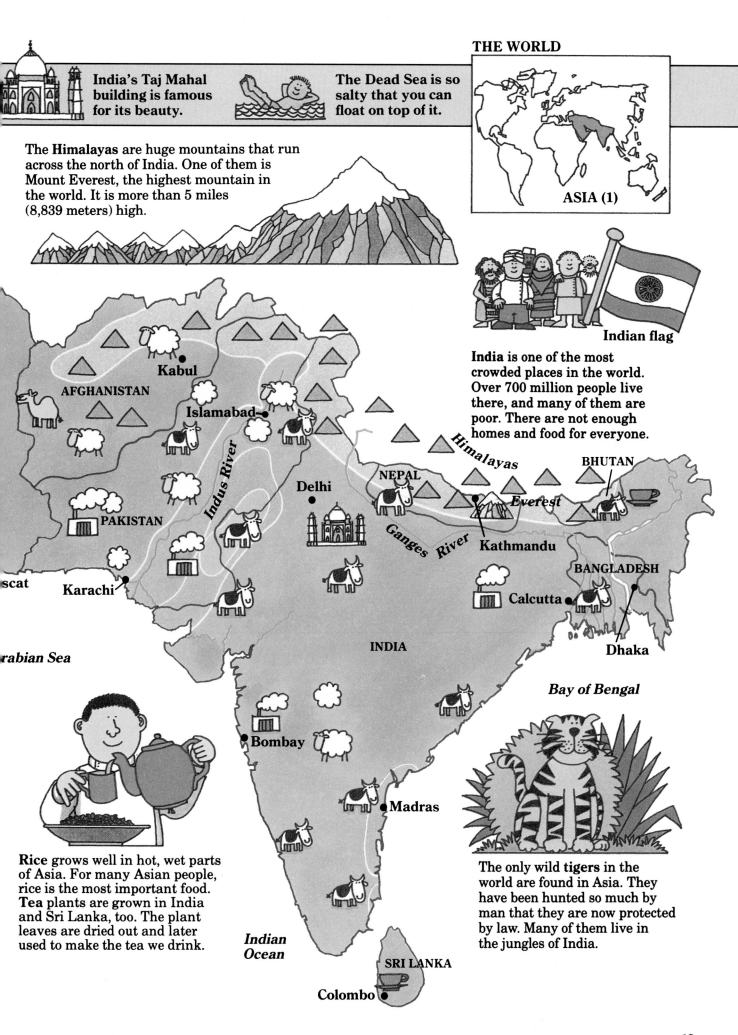

Indian flag

India is one of the most crowded places in the world. Over 700 million people live there, and many of them are poor. There are not enough homes and food for everyone.

AFGHANISTAN

Kabul

Islamabad

Indus River

PAKISTAN

Delhi

NEPAL

Himalayas

Everest

Kathmandu

Ganges River

BHUTAN

Karachi

scat

rabian Sea

Calcutta

BANGLADESH

Dhaka

INDIA

Bay of Bengal

Bombay

Madras

Rice grows well in hot, wet parts of Asia. For many Asian people, rice is the most important food. **Tea** plants are grown in India and Sri Lanka, too. The plant leaves are dried out and later used to make the tea we drink.

Indian Ocean

SRI LANKA

Colombo

The only wild **tigers** in the world are found in Asia. They have been hunted so much by man that they are now protected by law. Many of them live in the jungles of India.

Asia (2)

This map shows the rest of Asia, including China and Japan. There are many islands in the ocean around this part of Asia. It is sometimes called the Far East.

China's capital is the ancient city of Beijing.

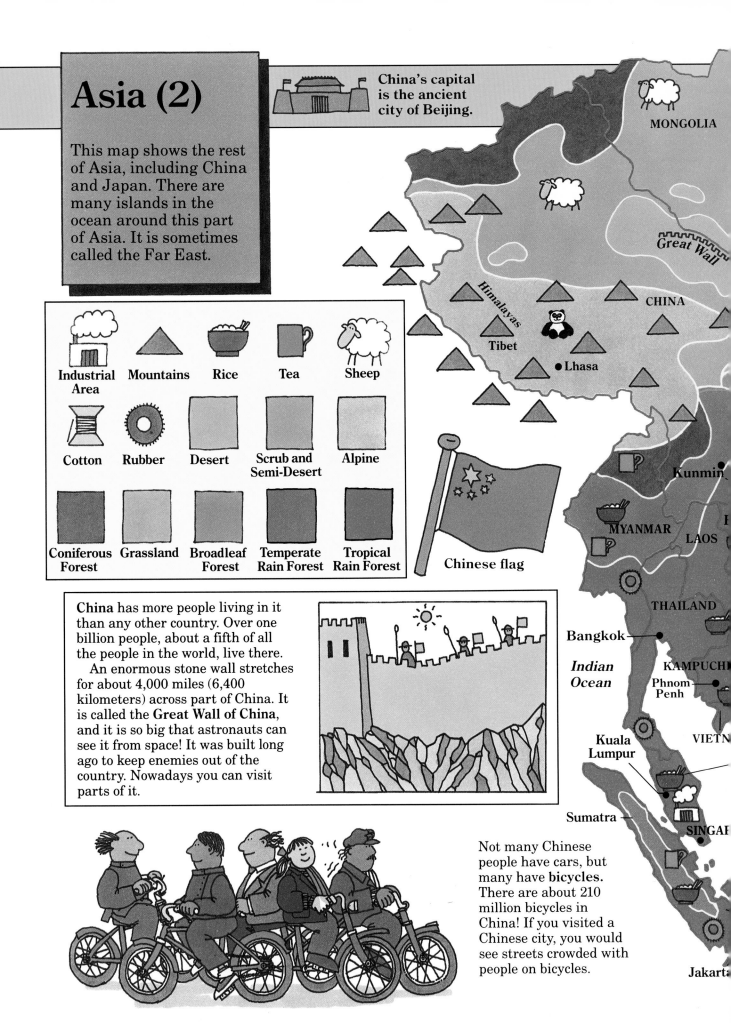

Key

Industrial Area
Mountains
Rice
Tea
Sheep
Cotton
Rubber
Desert
Scrub and Semi-Desert
Alpine
Coniferous Forest
Grassland
Broadleaf Forest
Temperate Rain Forest
Tropical Rain Forest

Chinese flag

MONGOLIA

Great Wall

Himalayas

Tibet

Lhasa

CHINA

Kunmin

MYANMAR

LAOS

THAILAND

Bangkok

Indian Ocean

KAMPUCHI

Phnom Penh

VIETN

Kuala Lumpur

Sumatra

SINGAF

Jakart

China has more people living in it than any other country. Over one billion people, about a fifth of all the people in the world, live there.

An enormous stone wall stretches for about 4,000 miles (6,400 kilometers) across part of China. It is called the **Great Wall of China**, and it is so big that astronauts can see it from space! It was built long ago to keep enemies out of the country. Nowadays you can visit parts of it.

Not many Chinese people have cars, but many have **bicycles**. There are about 210 million bicycles in China! If you visited a Chinese city, you would see streets crowded with people on bicycles.

The rare giant panda comes from China.

Harbin

Hokkaido

Honshu

Beijing

NORTH KOREA

JAPAN

Tianjin

Mount Fuji

Tokyo

SOUTH KOREA

Huang He River

Nanjing

Shikoku

Shanghai

Kyushu

g Jiang River

Japanese flag

ngzhou

Macao

Hong Kong

TAIWAN

Hainan

South China Sea

Manila

Chi
h City

PHILIPPINES

LAYSIA

BRUNEI

Pacific Ocean

Sarawak

Borneo

Sulawesi

INDONESIA

Java

Lesser Sunda Islands

Japan is made up of four large islands and about 3,000 small ones. Most Japanese people live on the four large islands: Hokkaido, Honshu, Shikoku, and Kyushu.

Most of the country is covered in forest and mountains. Some of the mountains are volcanoes, including famous Mount Fuji, which is inactive.

Mount Fuji

Tokyo is the capital of Japan. Along with Yokohama, it is the most populated area in the world. About 30 million people live in or near it.

Japan is a very rich country. It has many **factories** that make TVs, computers, cars, cameras, radios, and other machinery. Japan sells its products all over the world.

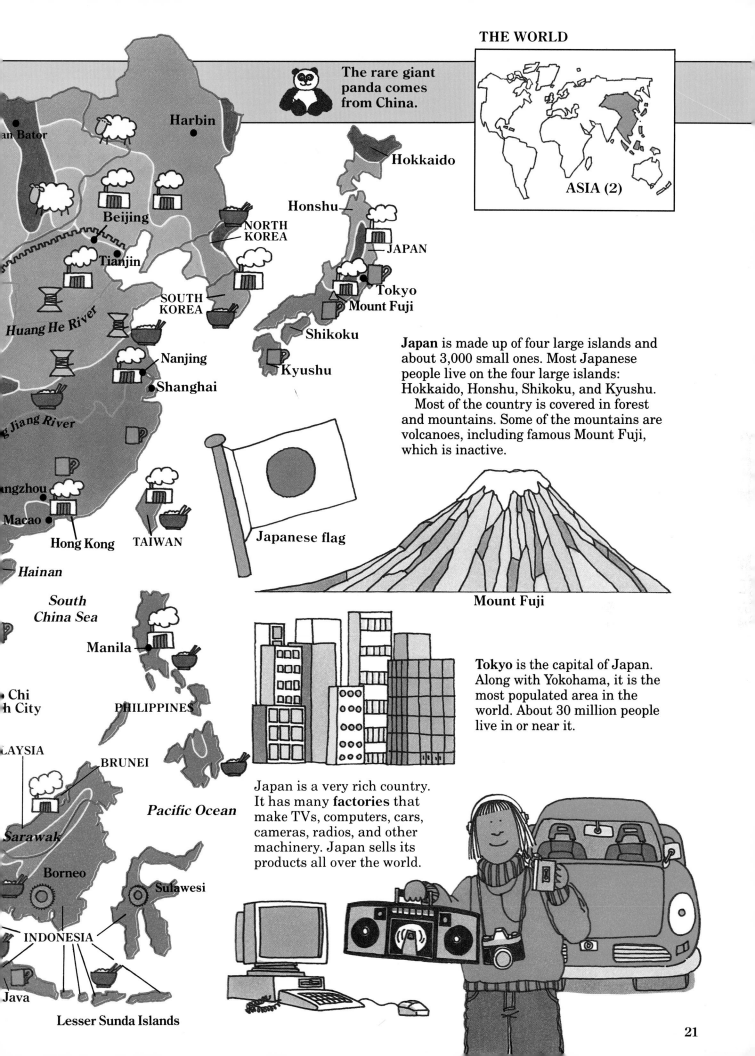

Australia and New Zealand

Australia is the smallest continent. About four fifths of it is covered in desert. New Zealand is made up of two large islands and several small ones. New Guinea is the world's second largest island.

 Ayers Rock is a large rock in the middle of Australia.

Australia has a coral reef called the Great Barrier Reef

There are many large **sheep farms** in Australia. The sheep provide people with meat and wool.

Darwin

The first people to live in Australia were **aborigines.** They gathered nuts and berries and hunted animals for food. There are still some aborigine tribes living in parts of Australia.

Indian Ocean

Northern Terr

Western Australia

AUSTRALIA

Australia has some unusual animals that are not found anywhere else in the world. Here are some examples:

Kangaroos carry their babies in pouches.

Furry **koalas** live in trees.

Australian flag

Perth

Great Australian B

The **duck-billed platypus** has fur and a beak like a duck.

The east coast of Australia has the most rainfall. Many of the **cities** are there.

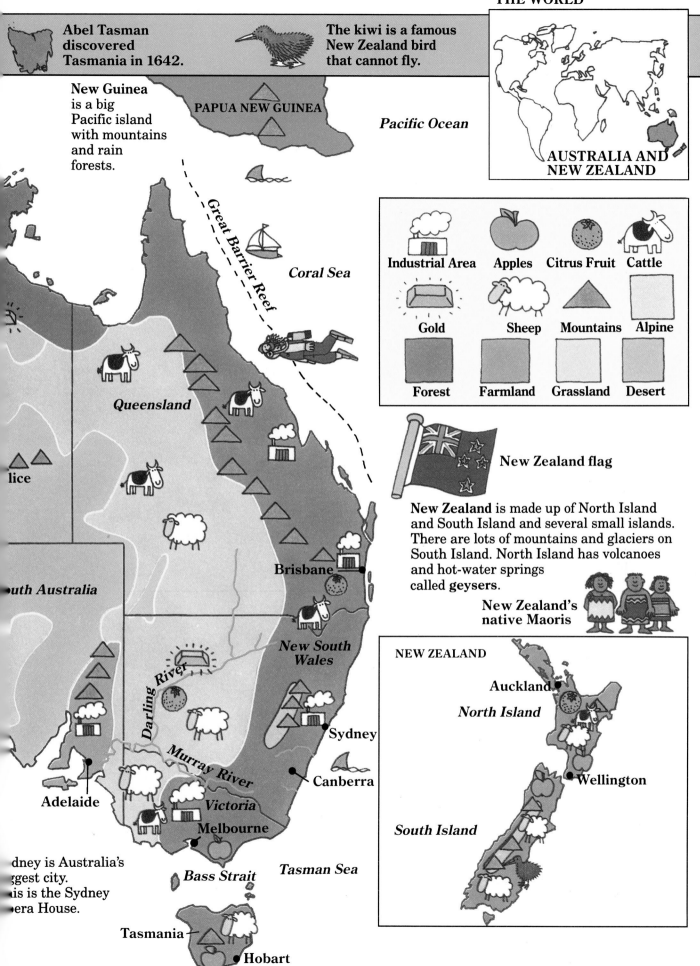

Abel Tasman discovered Tasmania in 1642.

The kiwi is a famous New Zealand bird that cannot fly.

THE WORLD

AUSTRALIA AND NEW ZEALAND

New Guinea is a big Pacific island with mountains and rain forests.

PAPUA NEW GUINEA

Pacific Ocean

Great Barrier Reef

Coral Sea

Industrial Area   Apples   Citrus Fruit   Cattle

Gold   Sheep   Mountains   Alpine

Forest   Farmland   Grassland   Desert

New Zealand flag

New Zealand is made up of North Island and South Island and several small islands. There are lots of mountains and glaciers on South Island. North Island has volcanoes and hot-water springs called geysers.

New Zealand's native Maoris

Queensland

lice

uth Australia

Brisbane

New South Wales

Darling River

Sydney

Murray River

Canberra

Adelaide

Victoria

Melbourne

dney is Australia's gest city. is is the Sydney era House.

Bass Strait

Tasman Sea

Tasmania

Hobart

NEW ZEALAND

Auckland

North Island

Wellington

South Island

23

The Arctic and Antarctica

The Arctic is a cold area of land and sea at the top of the earth.

Antarctica is an area of frozen land at the bottom of the earth.

 The top and bottom of the earth are called the Poles.

Summer and **winter** each last for six months in polar regions.

THE WORLD

ARCTIC

ANTARCTICA

Polar bears

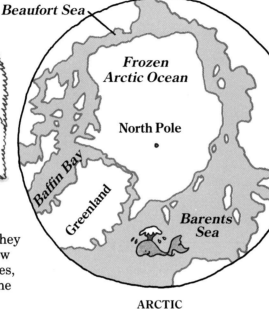

Beaufort Sea

Frozen Arctic Ocean

North Pole

Baffin Bay

Greenland

Barents Sea

ARCTIC

Many **Arctic animals** only visit in summer, when parts of the land are free of snow. When winter comes, they move farther south or burrow underground. A few creatures, such as polar bears, brave the winter blizzards.

The **Inuit** are a native people of the Arctic. Once they lived in igloos, dome-shaped huts made from ice. They hunted animals and traveled in sleds. Nowadays most of them live in modern settlements and travel on snowmobiles.

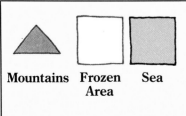

Scientists visit Antarctica to study the land. They stay in **research stations**.

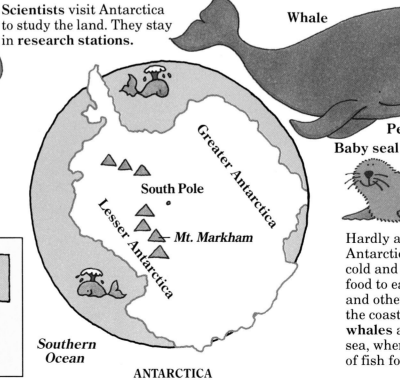

Whale

Penguin

Baby seal

South Pole

Greater Antarctica

Lesser Antarctica

Mt. Markham

Southern Ocean

ANTARCTICA

Mountains **Frozen Area** **Sea**

Hardly any **animals** live in Antarctica because it is too cold and there is almost no food to eat. But **penguins** and other birds live around the coasts. There are also **whales** and **seals** in the sea, where there are plenty of fish for them to eat.

24

What are you waiting for?
Head on over to
Atlas Fun,
starting on the next page…

A Flurry of Flags

Can you match the right flag with the right country? Below are twelve country names. Beneath them are eight numbered pictures of country flags you've seen in the atlas. On a separate piece of paper, write down the numbers 1 to 8. Then write the correct name of the country beside each number.

Italy	Canada	Japan
Mexico	Australia	Saudi Arabia
USA	Spain	India
USSR	Switzerland	Israel

World Record Holders

There are a number of fascinating "world records" that you've read about in *My First Atlas.* How many do you remember? On a separate piece of paper, write down the words that fill in the blanks of the following "world records." The first letter of each answer is in dark print to help you.

1. The largest desert in the world is the **S**_____ in North Africa.
2. The heaviest bird of prey in the world is the Andean **c**_____.
3. The highest mountain in the world is Mount **E**_____ in southern Asia.
4. The deepest lake in the world is Lake **B**_____ in the USSR.
5. The most populated area in the world is **T**_____ and Yokohama, Japan.

Atlas Fun

Do You Know Where You Are?

Pretend you're in the places pictured and described below. Can you answer the questions about where you are? Choose from the list underneath. Then write your answers on a blank piece of paper.

1. In looking down from the top of the 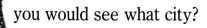 you would see what city?

2. You may meet up with a fierce  fish if you swim in what river?

3. If you see a  in the wild, you're on what island off the coast of Africa?

4. Walking along the 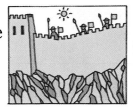 is a great thrill when visiting what country?

London	Rhine	Netherlands	Paris
Hokkaido	Antarctica	Madagascar	Australia
New Zealand	Amazon	Stockholm	China

M's and N's

In the United States of America, there are eight states starting with the letter M and eight states starting with the letter N. Can you name them all? The first two letters of each state name are given below. Write down your answers on a blank piece of paper.

Ma___   Mi_____   Ne_____   Ne_ _____
Ma_____   Mi_____   Ne____   Ne_ ____
Ma_____   Mi_____   Ne_ _____   No___ _____
Mi_____   Mo_____   Ne_ _____   No___ _____

Atlas Fun

Pen Pal Pictures

Pretend that a pen pal from Spain has sent you pictures (shown below) from foreign countries she's visited, including the USA. But she has forgotten to write the name of the country on the back of each picture. Can you tell in what country each of these pictures was taken? Write your answers on a separate piece of paper.

Your Spanish pen pal also visited one other country. But she forgot to send along a picture or tell you the name of the country. The first letters of the last six country names above, however, happen to spell the name of that extra country. What is it? Where is it?

Atlas Fun

Answers

A Flurry of Flags

1. Switzerland; 2. USA; 3. Japan; 4. Australia; 5. Mexico; 6. Canada; 7. Spain; 8. Italy

World Record Holders

1. Sahara; 2. condor; 3. Everest; 4. Baikal; 5. Tokyo

Do You Know Where You Are?

1. The picture is of the Eiffel Tower, so you're looking at the city of **Paris**.
2. The picture is of a piranha fish, so you'd be swimming in the **Amazon** River.
3. The picture is of a lemur, so you'd be on the island of **Madagascar**.
4. The picture is of the Great Wall of China, so you're in **China**.

M's and N's

Maine	Minnesota	Nebraska	New Mexico
Maryland	Mississippi	Nevada	New York
Massachusetts	Missouri	New Hampshire	North Carolina
Michigan	Montana	New Jersey	North Dakota

Pen Pal Pictures

1. The pyramids are in **E**gypt.
2. The rare giant panda is in **C**hina.
3. The Acropolis building is in **G**reece.
4. The Golden Gate Bridge is in the **U**nited States of America.
5. This gondola is on a canal in Venice, a city in **I**taly.
6. Maoris are native to **N**ew Zealand.
7. The Tower of London is in **E**ngland.
8. The platypus is found only in **A**ustralia.

The first letters of the last six country names above spell **Guinea.** It is a country in the west of Africa.

Index